MODERN AMERICAN INDIAN LEADERS

MASON CREST PUBLISHERS
PHILADELPHIA

Charles Barkley
Halle Berry
Cesar Chavez
Kenny Chesney
George Clooney
Johnny Depp
Tony Dungy
Jermaine Dupri
Jennifer Garner
Kevin Garnett
John B. Herrington
Salma Hayek
Vanessa Hudgens
Samuel L. Jackson
Norah Jones
Martin Lawrence
Bruce Lee
Eva Longoria
Malcolm X
Carlos Mencia
Chuck Norris
Barack Obama
Rosa Parks
Bill Richardson
Russell Simmons
Carrie Underwood
Modern American Indian Leaders

MODERN AMERICAN INDIAN LEADERS

RUTH HULL CHATLIEN

MASON CREST PUBLISHERS
PHILADELPHIA

ABOUT CROSS-CURRENTS

When you see this logo, turn to the Cross-Currents section at the back of the book. The Cross-Currents features explore connections between people, places, events, and ideas.

Produced by OTTN Publishing, Stockton, New Jersey

Mason Crest Publishers
370 Reed Road
Broomall, PA 19008
www.masoncrest.com

Printed and bound in the United States.

First printing

1 3 5 7 9 8 6 4 2

Library of Congress Cataloging-in-Publication Data

Chatlien, Ruth Hull.
Modern American Indian leaders / Ruth Hull Chatlien.
p. cm. — (Sharing the American dream)
Includes index.
ISBN 978-1-4222-0592-1 — ISBN 978-1-4222-0757-4 (pbk.)
1. Indians of North America—Government relations—Juvenile literature. 2. Indians of North America—Politics and government—Juvenile literature. 3. Indians of North America—Biography—Juvenile literature. 4. Political leadership—United States—Juvenile literature. I. Title.
E93.C43 2008
323.1197—dc22

2008024542

TABLE OF CONTENTS

CHAPTER ONE

AMERICAN INDIANS TODAY

On August 10, 2007, members of more than 250 American Indian tribes gathered at a large arena in Washington, D.C., for the third National Powwow. At noon, nearly 500 dancers entered the arena. They were dressed in a rainbow of colors. Their costumes featured feathers, fringe, and beadwork. They also wore moccasins and headbands.

The contests soon began. Men, women, and children competed in displays of traditional and modern styles of Indian dancing. Drummers and singers provided the music. Fringe and ribbons flew as the dancers whirled. Their feet moved in time to the booming beat of the drums.

In addition to dance and drum contests, the powwow honored American Indians who served in the armed forces. The gathering paid tribute to veterans of the wars in Iraq and Afghanistan, Operation Desert Storm (also known as the Gulf War), the Vietnam War, the Korean War, and World War II.

READ MORE
For a brief look at how the powwow has evolved, turn to page 44.

Many Different Tribes

A large number of Native Americans still live in North

An American Indian musical group competes in a drumming contest during the final day of the third National Powwow, Washington, D.C., August 12, 2007.

America. In the 2001 Canadian census, more than a million people reported having native ancestry. According to the U.S. Census Bureau, in the year 2000 about 2.5 million people reported having American Indian or Alaska Native ancestry. The largest tribes were the Cherokee, Navajo, Choctaw, Blackfeet, Chippewa, Muscogee, Apache,

READ MORE

Determining who can claim membership in a particular tribe isn't always straightforward. See page 45 for details.

and Lumbee, with more than 50,000 members each. Here is some information about these tribes:

- The Cherokee were originally from the Appalachian Mountain region. They lived in towns and farmed. In the 1830s, the U.S. government forced them to move to Oklahoma.

- The Navajo are a people of the Southwest. Many are farmers. They are known for making fine crafts such as rugs and silver jewelry.

- The Choctaws originally lived in southeast Mississippi. Although they had to move to Oklahoma in the 1830s, some later returned to their homeland.

(Above) A Cherokee man dressed in traditional clothing. (Left) A young Navajo performs a ceremonial dance.

• The Blackfeet live in Montana and Canada. Originally, they were a nation of hunters and strong warriors. Later they became farmers and ranchers.

• The Chippewa are also known as the Ojibwe or the Anishinaabe. They live in the north-central United States and in Canada. Their way of life included hunting and gathering wild rice.

• The Muscogee are a branch of the Creek Indians. They lived and farmed in the Southeast. They were forced to move to Oklahoma in the 1830s.

• The Apache live in the Southwest. They were once warriors who lived by hunting and raiding. They fought fiercely to avoid staying on reservations, but eventually lost.

• The Lumbee live in North Carolina. The tribe is recognized by the state but not by the U.S. government.

Today American Indians lead lives that blend old and new ways. Many have moved to cities and work at modern jobs. In the book *Native America Today*, author Barry M. Pritzker explained:

> Many Indians and Inuit (Eskimos) are also major players in local, regional, and national . . . decision making. In fact, native people today—teachers, lawyers, engineers, planners, artists, entrepreneurs, and others—influence life in North America to a degree not seen in centuries.

Other Indians live on reservations and work in traditional jobs such as farming or ranching. Even so, they are likely to use modern technology. Although the old ways of life have changed, many American Indians identify with their culture and do not want to lose it. They have struggled to keep their language and traditions alive.

Threats to Indian Culture

For most of the 1800s, many American Indian tribes fought to stop white settlers from taking their lands. The wars ended in 1890 when the U.S. army massacred more than 200 Sioux at Wounded Knee, South Dakota. Both during and after the Indian wars, the U.S. government took many actions to try to make Indians live the way that whites did.

First, beginning in the 1830s, most tribes were moved onto reservations, often far from their homelands. Indians believe that their land is owned by the whole tribe. Yet the government divided reservation lands and gave pieces to individuals. Owning land did not help Indians make a good living. In almost all cases, reservation lands were poor and difficult to farm.

Second, from the mid-1800s to the mid-1900s, Indian children were taken from their families and sent to boarding schools. At those schools, children were forced to give up Indian clothes, language, and religion. Often they were not allowed to see their families. At the boarding schools, children suffered loneliness, shame, and abusive punishment. Even after they left school, many experienced problems as adults. Those problems included depression, substance abuse, poor parenting skills, and family violence. In a speech in 2000, Kevin Gover, an official of the Bureau of Indian Affairs (BIA), apologized for what had been done:

> Never again will we attack your religions, your languages, your rituals, or any of your tribal ways. Never again will we seize your children, nor teach them to be ashamed of who they are. Never again.

Third, the government tried to end support for tribes. In the past, when the United States took Indian lands, government and tribal leaders usually signed a treaty. In many cases, the treaties promised that the government would give money or help to the tribe. In the 1950s, the government wanted to stop giving that help. This change was called the termination policy.

At the same time, the government began to move many Indians to cities. The goal was for rural Indians to learn modern jobs so they would live like whites. The government promised them temporary housing, counseling, training, and help finding jobs. Those promises were not always kept. Many of the Indians who did find jobs ended up with unskilled work that paid little. Some returned to the reservations. Others stayed in the cities and began to band together to fight for Indian rights.

Keeping the Culture Alive

During the 1960s, American Indian leaders began to fight to save their culture. Some led protests to inform the American public about problems that American Indians faced. For example, Indians briefly occupied Alcatraz, an island near San Francisco, California, in 1964. They were protesting the loss of Indian lands.

Other American Indians fought for self-government and religious freedom. Some fought to gain economic rights. These included the right to open casinos on reservations or control fishing in their rivers and lakes. Many Indians worked to teach their children Indian languages so the culture wouldn't be lost. As the Lakota leader Russell Means explained in his autobiography, "We fought to instill pride in our songs and in our language, in our cultural wisdom."

Thanks to people like Russell Means and the other leaders you will read about in this book, American Indian culture is still alive—and flourishing—today.

CHAPTER TWO

BEN NIGHTHORSE CAMPBELL: A WARRIOR SENATOR

One night in 1991, when he was a congressman living in Washington, D.C., Ben Nighthorse Campbell walked to the grocery store. On his way home, he noticed a man following him. In a newspaper article in the *Pueblo Chieftain*, Ben explained, "Every time I stopped to look back at him, he would turn away and look in a store window. That set alarm bells ringing."

When the stranger demanded his money, Ben refused. The two started to fight. Ben fought off the would-be mugger, but because he injured his ankle, he couldn't give chase when the man ran away. "And I didn't want to leave my groceries," Ben noted. "In this town, they wouldn't have been there when I got back."

It might seem unusual for a 57-year-old lawmaker to beat off a robber. But Ben Nighthorse Campbell has a history of standing up for himself.

From Loner to Team Captain

Ben Campbell was born in 1933 in Auburn, California. His father, Albert Campbell, was a Northern Cheyenne Indian. His mother, Mary, was a Portuguese immigrant. Ben had an older sister named Alberta.

Wearing the full ceremonial dress of his Northern Cheyenne tribe, Senator Ben Nighthorse Campbell attends the ground breaking for the Smithsonian Institution's National Museum of the American Indian, September 1999.

Albert Campbell was an alcoholic who sometimes had no job. Mary developed a disease called tuberculosis and was often in the hospital. Because of the family's problems, Ben and Alberta lived in an orphanage for a while. Even when they were home, life was difficult. In an article in *People* magazine, Ben explained, "I remember being so . . . poor that my mother would split a can of peas between my sister and me. She didn't eat anything. All she had was the juice from the bottom of the can."

At school, Ben did not earn good grades or get along with other students. By high school, he was getting into trouble by drinking, fighting, and stealing cars. He dropped out when he was 17. He worked in logging camps and saw himself as a loner.

Then, in the late 1940s, Ben found a place where he felt he belonged. While working in a fruit-packing plant, he argued with a Japanese coworker. When they fought, the other man used judo to defeat Ben. Eventually, the two young men became friends, and Ben started to learn judo himself. The martial art helped him learn discipline. Even though Ben did not go back to high school, he settled down. While working odd jobs, he continued to practice judo and improve his skills.

For information about what judo is and how it developed, see page 46.

In 1951, Ben joined the U.S. Air Force. He served in Korea until 1954. While in the service, he earned his GED. When he returned to the United States, he enrolled at San Jose State University. There he earned a degree in physical education and fine arts.

From 1960 to 1964, Ben lived in Japan and studied judo. He won a gold medal at the Pan American Games in 1963. He also became the captain of the 1964 U.S. Olympic judo team. Unluckily, he injured his knee during a match and could not earn a medal. However, his teammates respected him so much that they chose Ben to carry the U.S. flag at the closing ceremony.

Putting Down Roots

After his knee injury, Ben was no longer able to compete in judo matches. He began to teach the sport. During one of his classes, he met a teacher named Linda Price, who was originally from Colorado. They married in 1966. Linda was Ben's third wife. His first marriage had been annulled, and his second marriage ended in divorce.

Linda and Ben had two children—a son named Colin and a daughter named Shanan. In 1979, the family moved to a ranch in Colorado. Ben earned a living by designing and selling jewelry. His jewelry earned many awards.

In 1980, Ben enrolled as a member of the Northern Cheyenne tribe. At that time, he added Nighthorse to his name. The name honors one of Ben's ancestors—Ruben Black Horse, who fought in the Battle of the Little Bighorn. In 1985, Ben Nighthorse Campbell was elected to the Northern Cheyenne's Council of 44 Chiefs.

READ MORE

In 1876, Sioux and Cheyenne Indians defeated Seventh Cavalry troops led by George Custer at the Little Bighorn River. For more information on the famous battle, see page 47.

Entering Politics

Ben never intended to have a political career. In 1982, he happened to attend a meeting of the Colorado Democratic Party, which was trying to choose a candidate for the state legislature. After several people had turned down requests to run, the party asked Ben. He agreed when party officials told him it wouldn't be much work. To everyone's surprise, Ben won the election. He served as a state representative for four years.

In 1986, Colorado voters elected Ben to the U.S. House of Representatives. At the time, he was the only Native American in Congress. He was a colorful figure who wore a ponytail, a bolo tie, and cowboy boots. He also rode a motorcycle.

While he was in the House, Ben fought for Indian interests. He opposed a plan to close the Bureau of Indian Affairs. He succeeded in having the Custer Battlefield in Montana renamed the Little Bighorn National Monument. Ben objected to the old name because Indians, not Custer, had won the battle. Ben sponsored a bill to create the National Museum of the American Indian. The

Shortly after winning a seat in the U.S. Senate, Ben Nighthorse Campbell greets a well-wisher, November 13, 1992. He would go on to serve two terms in the Senate.

bill was signed into law in 1989. Another of his causes was preventing fetal alcohol syndrome. Babies with this syndrome can have problems such as low birth weight and brain damage. It occurs when a woman drinks alcohol during pregnancy.

Ben was elected to the U.S. Senate in 1992. He continued to be different from other members of Congress—and not just because of the way he dressed. His opinions didn't totally match the views of either political party. Like the Democrats he represented, he was liberal on many social issues. Yet like Republicans,

Ben Nighthorse Campbell speaks at a White House ceremony celebrating the opening of the National Museum of the American Indian, September 23, 2004. President George W. Bush is at right.

he was conservative on economic issues. For example, he supported ranching, mining, and timber interests. As time went on, he found that he disagreed more often with the Democrats. For one thing, he thought the government spent too much money. In 1995, he switched parties and became a Republican.

In 1996, Ben became the chairman of the Senate Committee on Indian Affairs. He was the first American Indian to hold that position. As part of his work, he tried to improve health and education on reservations. He sought to protect Indian water rights and other resources.

Ben was reelected to the U.S. Senate in 1998. Toward the end of that six-year term, he was treated for prostate cancer. In 2004, he decided not to run again because of his health.

After leaving politics, Ben returned to jewelry making. He has also served as a policy adviser to a law firm active in political lobbying.

CHAPTER THREE

ADA DEER: THE WOMAN WHO TOOK ON CONGRESS

In 1992, a newspaper photograph showed an American Indian woman holding a sign that said, "Me Nominee." The slogan was a play on words. The woman in the photo was Ada Deer, a member of the Menominee tribe of Wisconsin. The sign was using the name of her tribe to announce that she was the Democratic nominee, or candidate, for U.S. Congress. Ada Deer was the first American Indian woman to run for Congress. Throughout her life, she has been a trailblazer, making history for her people.

Ada Deer, a member of the Menominee tribe, became the first woman to head the Bureau of Indian Affairs.

Raised to Succeed

In 1935, Ada was born in Keshena, Wisconsin, on the Menominee reservation. Her father, Joseph, was a Menominee. Her mother, Constance, was a white nurse who cared deeply about Indian rights.

The family lived in a log cabin without electricity or running water. Yet Ada loved where she lived. She explained her love of nature in her essay "The Menominee Quest":

> Like my ancestors before me, I absorbed a deep love and respect for the land and for all living things—trees, plants, and birds, to name but a few. This legacy, so precious to all of us, is central to being Indian. This kinship with the land . . . is a driving force in tribal life.

In 1940, Ada's family moved to Milwaukee, the largest city in Wisconsin. Her parents wanted to earn more money. Not long afterward, the United States began fighting in World War II. Joseph Deer was drafted into the army. In Milwaukee, Ada and her siblings were the only Indian children in their neighborhood. Other children often fought with them because they were different.

When Ada was 10, one of her brothers became sick, so the family returned to the reservation. The fresh air and milk from the family's goats helped the boy get better. Ada attended a public school in a nearby town. Once again, she felt that her classmates looked down on her. Even so, she studied hard because her mother pushed her to succeed.

After Ada graduated from high school, she enrolled at the University of Wisconsin. The Menominee tribe helped pay her tuition by giving her $1,000 a year. Her goal was to go to medical school after college.

READ MORE

The log cabin has become a popular symbol of frontier life during the 19th century. But this simple dwelling, which could be constructed without nails, was actually introduced to North America much earlier. For details, see page 48.

After her freshman year, Ada went to New York on a summer program to study democracy. While there, she met former first lady Eleanor Roosevelt. Shortly afterward, she decided she wanted to study social work instead of medicine.

READ MORE

Meeting Eleanor Roosevelt made a big impression on Ada Deer. For a profile of Mrs. Roosevelt, who was widely admired for her humanitarian work, turn to page 49.

Ada earned her undergraduate degree from the University of Wisconsin in 1957. She was awarded a master's degree from Columbia University in 1961. After finishing her education, Ada worked in Minneapolis, Minnesota, with urban Indians. Later, she worked as a school social worker. In 1969, Ada moved back to her home state to head a program at the University of Wisconsin. Ada also did volunteer work. For example, she served on the board of directors for the Girl Scouts.

Fighting for Menominee Rights

During the 1950s, the federal government began the termination program. This was an effort to end government support for Indian tribes. One of the first groups the government targeted was the Menominee tribe.

Ada Deer, chairperson of the Menominee Restoration Committee, January 1973. Later that year, the U.S. government restored the Menominees' official tribal status.

In the early 1950s, the Menominees were one of the wealthiest Indian tribes. The reservation had a hospital. It had its own electric company. The Menominees also owned a sawmill, which provided many people with jobs.

The tribe should have had another source of income. It had successfully brought a lawsuit against the government, winning a settlement of several million dollars. However, an official falsely claimed that the tribe could collect the payments only if it agreed to termination. A majority of the tribe's members were fooled, and they voted to approve termination.

Termination took place in 1961. It proved to be a disaster for the Menominees. The hospital closed, and the electric plant was sold. The tribe no longer received help from the Bureau of Indian Affairs. As a result, people had to pay for services that used to be free. Also, Menominee lands stopped being a reservation. Because of that, many people had to buy the land where they lived.

Operations at the sawmill changed too. New managers took over and tried to make the mill earn more money. They fired many Menominees and replaced them with machines. By 1970, the Menominee people were struggling with poverty.

The Menominees' sawmill provided many members of the tribe with jobs. Unfortunately, termination brought new management to the mill, and many workers were laid off.

A small group of people, some of them non-Indians, ran the tribe. They decided to sell land for a vacation-home development. The plan included construction of dams to create an artificial body of water, Legend Lake, from nine natural lakes. The majority of Menominees opposed the development plan. In "The Menominee Quest," Ada Deer explained their feelings: "Like me, other Menominees were wounded to the heart when, unannounced, bulldozers began slashing and clearing trees from our beautiful lake shores and slicing the land into lots to be sold."

Ada decided to take action. With other leaders, she founded a group called DRUMS, which stood for Determination of Rights and Unity for Menominee Stockholders. This group wanted to stop the Legend Lake project. To do that, they worked to give the majority of the Menominees more say in their government. DRUMS managed to take over the Menominees' ruling body and prevent more damage to the land.

DRUMS members also wanted to repeal termination. They hoped to restore the Menominee tribe to official status, so it could receive BIA help again. Ada spent two years in Washington, D.C., urging Congress to restore the tribe's status. One of her friends told her she would never succeed. But in 1973, a law was passed that made the Menominees an official tribe again.

Continuing to Work for Indians

Because of her work for the tribe, Ada was chosen to be the first woman to lead the Menominees. She served in this role from 1974 to 1976. After that, she twice ran for Wisconsin secretary of state, but she was defeated each time. She also lost her 1992 campaign for Congress.

In 1993, President Bill Clinton appointed Ada to the post of assistant secretary for Indian Affairs. This made her the head

After leaving government service, Ada Deer returned to the University of Wisconsin, where she has taught in the American Indian Studies Program and the School of Social Work.

of the BIA, the first Indian woman to hold that job. Under her leadership, 223 Alaskan villages and 12 Indian tribes gained official status. Congress passed several laws protecting Indian rights. Ada resigned from the BIA in 1997. The government was trying to cut costs, and her support for Indian programs went against that policy.

Since then, Ada has taught at the University of Wisconsin at Madison, where she headed the American Indian Studies Program. In 2007, the Wisconsin Historical Society honored her for a lifetime of public service.

CHAPTER FOUR

WINONA LaDUKE: CANDIDATE FOR VICE PRESIDENT

In 1996 and 2000, an Anishinaabe activist named Winona LaDuke was a candidate for vice president of the United States. Winona and presidential candidate Ralph Nader ran on the Green Party's ticket. The Green Party is much smaller than either the Democratic or Republican parties.

During the 2000 campaign, Winona and Nader focused on many issues. They spoke about fighting poverty, providing health care, and getting rid of special advantages for big businesses. Many people criticized the two for being in the election. Critics claimed that they took votes away from the Democratic candidate, Al Gore, and caused George W. Bush to win.

READ MORE

For a profile of Ralph Nader, Winona LaDuke's Green Party running mate in the 1996 and 2000 presidential campaigns, see page 50.

Winona disagreed. In *The Winona LaDuke Reader,* she pointed out that nearly half of all Americans don't bother to vote because they have lost interest.

> America is the single most difficult democracy in the world in which to participate. And, fewer and

> fewer people do. The reality is that the largest party in America is neither the Democrats nor the Republicans—the largest party is the non-voters.

Winona believed that she and Ralph Nader gave voters an alternative to the stale policies of the Democratic and Republican parties.

Indian rights activist Winona LaDuke twice ran for vice president of the United States. LaDuke and her Green Party running mate, Ralph Nader, emphasized social justice, fair trade, and environmental sustainability.

A Political Childhood

Both of Winona's parents were interested in politics. Her mother, Betty, is a painter of Russian-Jewish descent. She uses her art to celebrate cultures around the world. Winona's father, Vincent, was an Anishinaabe actor. He also worked as an Indian rights activist, trying to make the government honor treaties.

Winona was born in 1959 in Los Angeles, California. Her parents divorced five years later, and Winona moved to Ashland, Oregon, with her mother. Almost everyone was white, and Winona had a hard time fitting in there. In school, she wasn't invited to dances or asked to join sports teams. She did become involved with her high school debate team. Competing in speech contests taught her skills she would later use as a public speaker.

Winona's guidance counselor suggested that she train for a trade after high school. Instead, she wanted a college education. She was accepted at Harvard, one of the finest universities in the country. While there, she made Indian friends and worked on environmental issues. Winona graduated with a degree in economics. She later earned a master's degree.

In 1982, Winona moved to the White Earth Reservation in Minnesota to work as a high school principal. The reservation was where her father had grown up, but Winona had never lived there. She did not speak the language or know anyone. Some people viewed her as an outsider. Even so, she became involved in political issues.

Living on the Reservation

The 1867 treaty that created the White Earth Reservation set aside 837,000 acres for the Anishinaabe. Over time, many Indians lost land because they couldn't afford their taxes. Others were pressured to sell in deals that may not have been legal. By the late 1900s, the tribe had lost 90 percent of its land to non-Indians—lumber companies, local governments, farmers, and others. Winona and other Indians filed a lawsuit to try to regain those lands.

The lawsuit failed, but Winona didn't give up. She had received a $20,000 prize for working to promote human rights. Instead of keeping the money, she used it to start the White Earth Land Recovery Project (WELRP) in 1989. The group's goal is to return reservation lands to Anishinaabe ownership. By the first years of the 21st century, about 1,300 acres had been regained through purchase and donation.

The WELRP also seeks to restore the ecosystems on reservation lands. For example, the group wants to stop lumber companies from cutting down entire forests. Instead, the WELRP advocates cutting only some trees at a time, so the forest remains intact. Winona believes that Indians and lumber companies view the forest differently. The lumber companies see only timber to be sold. The Indians feel connected to the living trees. In *The Winona LaDuke Reader,* Winona explained, "Who we are is our land, our trees, and our lakes. This is central to our local and collective work. This is also why the conflict remains in Native America between corporate interests and our traditional ways."

In 1982, Winona attended an Indian conference in Ontario, Canada. While she was there, she met Randy Kapashesit. He was a representative of the Cree, a Canadian tribe. The two married in 1988 and had a daughter and a son. Winona continued to live in Minnesota and Randy lived in Ontario. They visited each other but found it too difficult to maintain a close relationship that way. They separated in 1992. Later, Winona formed a relationship with Kevin Gasco, her business partner. The two have a son.

Last Standing Woman

Winona's organization, the WELRP, started businesses to help Indians earn a living on the reservation. The traditional Anishinaabe way of life involves gathering wild rice, which is native to parts of Canada and the north-central United States, including Minnesota. The WELRP operates a mill and a store to sell the wild rice. It also runs a coffee-roasting business.

Recently, Winona launched a campaign to protect wild rice. Scientists are working to create genetically modified crops that are hardier or more productive than traditional varieties. But genetically modified crops can cause problems. If their pollen reaches wild plants, the wild plants will produce seeds that grow a different variety. Native varieties might disappear because their seeds will be corrupted. Because of that, Winona wants lawmakers to keep genetically modified wild rice out of Minnesota.

Winona works for causes off the reservation, too. She founded an organization called the Indigenous Women's Network. This

Winona LaDuke speaks at a rally protesting the University of Minnesota's involvement in mapping the genetic sequence of wild rice, May 2002. She is concerned that biotech companies might genetically modify wild rice, which is sacred to American Indian cultures.

group supports native women around the world as they work for their communities. Winona spoke at the World Conference on Women in Beijing in 1995. She has also been in several documentaries and one feature film.

In addition to being an activist, Winona is a writer. She has written many newspaper and magazine articles. She wrote a novel called *Last Standing Woman*, which is based partially on her life. Even though she was not elected vice president, Winona LaDuke continues to be a woman who stands tall and speaks out for Indian rights.

CHAPTER FIVE

PHILLIP MARTIN: LEADING HIS PEOPLE TO PROSPERITY

After growing up in extreme poverty on a reservation in Mississippi, Choctaw leader Phillip Martin was drafted into the military. World War II had just ended. "I joined the Army Air Forces in August 1945 and went to Europe during the occupation. We were replacements for GIs who were returning home," Phillip said in an article for the American Forces Press Service.

What he saw in Europe changed his life. Because of the massive bombing that took place during the war, many European cities were in ruins. Phillip saw starving people digging through garbage cans looking for food. For the first time, he realized that white people could be as poor as Indians. Yet he also saw something else that inspired him. Defeated Germans were searching through the rubble to find bricks that were still in one piece. They wanted to rebuild their bombed cities. If those people could work to lift themselves from poverty, Phillip wondered, why couldn't his Choctaw people do the same?

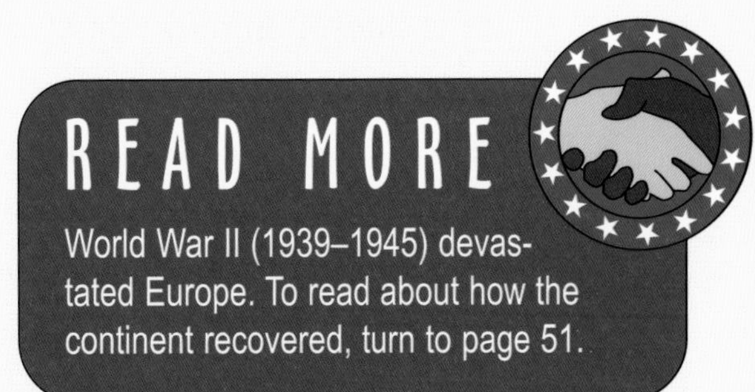

World War II (1939–1945) devastated Europe. To read about how the continent recovered, turn to page 51.

Inspired by efforts to rebuild Europe after World War II, Phillip Martin made it his life's work to help the Choctaw tribe rise from poverty.

That question would later guide him when he became leader of the Choctaws.

Overcoming Poverty

Phillip Martin was born in 1926. His mother, Mary, was a homemaker. His father, Willie, was a BIA janitor who died while Phillip was still a boy. Phillip had four brothers who also served in the armed forces, as well as one sister.

Life on the reservation was hard. The Choctaw reservation in Mississippi was considered the poorest section of one of the nation's poorest states. Homes had no windows, no electricity, and no plumbing. The reservation had no doctors. Few Choctaws received more than a grade-school education. The only jobs that were available were menial ones such as chopping wood, sweeping floors, or herding cows.

To make matters worse, the Choctaws faced constant discrimination. In Mississippi during the first half of the 20th century, Indians had to obey the same Jim Crow laws that restricted the rights of African Americans. They had to get off the sidewalk if a white person approached. They could not eat in the same restaurants or attend the same schools as whites. The Choctaws themselves had their own prejudices. When they were told to send their children to black public schools, the Choctaws chose to keep their children at home.

Phillip Martin was determined to do better for himself. To gain a high school education, he traveled to North Carolina when he was 13. There he attended a BIA boarding school. The school was for Cherokee students, and Phillip was the only Choctaw there. His previous schooling was so poor that he was placed in the fourth grade. In spite of that setback, he earned a high school diploma at age 18, completing eight years of schooling in only five years.

READ MORE

Jim Crow was the name given to a system of laws and practices that kept blacks separated from whites in the South. In some places, Jim Crow also affected Indians. For details, see page 52.

After joining the U.S. Army Air Forces, Phillip thought about having a military career. He stayed in the service for 10 years, served in Korea, and worked his way up to staff sergeant. Even though he liked being in the military, he decided that he might find more opportunity out of the service. His plan was to leave the reservation and move to a city like Chicago or San Francisco. He explained his reasons in an article for the American Forces Press Service:

> You have a lot of advantages in the military. You see the world, meet a lot of good people, have a lot of good comradeship, and you develop leadership. So I wasn't used to the way things were when I came home, and I was going to leave because I didn't think I could change anything.

Before leaving the reservation for good, Phillip returned to see his family in 1955. His plan for a short visit turned into a permanent stay. What changed his mind? He met a woman named Bonnie Bell and fell in love. She didn't want to leave her family, so Phillip remained in Mississippi. The couple married and had two daughters, Deborah and Patricia.

Chief of the Choctaws

Phillip had trouble finding work. So he took advantage of the G.I. Bill—a law that provided benefits for veterans—to pay for more schooling. He studied to be an electrician. Finally, in 1961, he found a job at the Meridian Naval Air Station.

In 1957, while Phillip was in school, he was elected to a seat on the Choctaw tribal council. Within a few years, Phillip had become chairman of the council. His salary as chairman was only $2.50 a week! At that time, the local BIA officials controlled the tribe's government. The BIA superintendent ran the council's meetings and guided members on trips to Washington. Phillip resented being treated like a child. "I've been all over the world. I guess I know how to go to Washington and back," he recalled years later. "From now on, we don't need the superintendent."

Phillip began to travel to Washington regularly, seeking money to help the Choctaws. During the 1960s, they received a Community Action Program grant of $15,000. They used the money to set up a management system. This system would make sure they used any other federal money they received efficiently.

Then the Choctaws received a grant to build an industrial park. Phillip contacted manufacturers, inviting them to locate a factory on the reservation. He had to write to more than 150 companies before he found one that would work with the Choctaws. The tribe built a factory and set to work making automobile parts. However, few Choctaws had experience with the discipline and routine of working every day. After a year, the business faced bankruptcy. Phillip hired an experienced plant manager to train his people, and the business began to succeed. Over time, the Choctaws invested in a variety of other businesses. The tribe's economic health grew stronger. Life on

Phillip Martin, chief of the Choctaws, listens to Cherokee Nation chief Wilma Mankiller at a 1989 congressional hearing. Phillip led the Choctaws from 1959 to 2007.

the reservation improved as the tribe built better homes, roads, schools, and a medical center.

Phillip served as chief of the Choctaws for more than 45 years. In 2007, another man was elected to the post. Content to accept his people's decision, Phillip Martin retired at the age of 81. During his time in office, he led his people out of crushing poverty and helped them become a model of success.

CHAPTER SIX

RUSSELL MEANS: PROTESTS AND CONTROVERSY

In the mid-1990s, Indian activist Russell Means did something that made critics accuse him of selling out to American pop culture. He provided the voice of Chief Powhatan in Disney's animated film *Pocahontas* (1995). The movie tells the story of conflict between early American settlers in Jamestown, Virginia, and the Powhatan Indians who lived in that area. Means, known for his angry criticism of the U.S. government and its treatment of Indians, defended his decision to appear in the movie. In an article in the magazine *The Santa Fean*, Means said, "Pocahontas is the finest movie ever made about American Indians because it told the truth about the settlers at Jamestown. . . . It's the only movie about our women, how strong they are. They are the true leaders of Indian people!"

Many people consider Means a leader of the Lakota, a Sioux people. Others think he is a troublemaker. He became famous for protesting the mistreatment of American Indians and remains a controversial figure today.

Growing up Tough

Russell Means was born on an Indian reservation in South Dakota in 1939. His father, Hank, was a mixed-blood Sioux. His

Russell Means—activist, author, and actor—has had a remarkably varied career. The *Los Angeles Times* once described him as the most famous American Indian since Sitting Bull and Crazy Horse.

mother, Theodora, was a full-blooded Sioux. In the years after Russell's birth, his three younger brothers were born.

The family had problems. Theodora often became upset and whipped her children with a strap. Hank drank too much and sometimes spent the family's food money on alcohol.

In 1942, the Means family moved to Vallejo, California, because Hank and Theodora thought their children would have more opportunities there. The move had mixed results. Hank found work as a welder in a shipyard. However, the Means boys faced prejudice because few Indians lived in Vallejo.

In high school, Russell began to rebel. He got into fights. He often got drunk and took drugs. Even so, he managed to earn his diploma. Afterward, he worked at many different types of jobs. Some of these were ballroom dancer, janitor, and rodeo hand.

Meanwhile, he continued to drink and fight. Sometimes, he made money by gambling or cheating storeowners. He married and had a son, but the marriage quickly fell apart.

Russell's life changed because of a demonstration on the island of Alcatraz. Located near San Francisco, Alcatraz was the site of a closed federal prison. An old treaty gave the Sioux the right to take any federal lands that were no longer being used. In 1964, a group of Indians seized Alcatraz. The group included Russell's father, Hank Means, who invited Russell to take part.

The Indians did not win their fight to become owners of Alcatraz. Even so, the event was a turning point in Russell's life. It helped him take pride in being an Indian. It also made him want to continue to protest. He later said in his autobiography, *Where White Men Fear to Tread*, "It was my first inkling of what direct action can accomplish." From that point on, he was an activist for Indian rights.

Indians in the exercise yard at Alcatraz. A 1964 occupation of the closed federal prison facility inspired Russell Means to become an activist for Indian rights.

Standing up for Indians

In 1968, Russell and his second wife, Betty, moved to Cleveland, Ohio, with their children. He helped start the Cleveland American Indian Center. In 1969, he went to a conference in San Francisco and met the founders of the American Indian Movement (AIM). AIM was a civil rights group that focused on problems faced by

Indians. Russell joined the group in 1970 and started a chapter in Cleveland.

During the 1970s, Russell took part in many protests led by AIM. One of the most famous was called the Trail of Broken Treaties. In 1972, Indians from across the country went to Washington, D.C., to draw attention to all the promises that the U.S. government had broken. When they arrived in Washington, the protesters had trouble finding places to stay. Russell and other demonstrators went to the headquarters of the BIA and took over the building. The Indians stayed there for seven days. During that time, officials agreed to look into their complaints. Even though the protesters damaged the building and destroyed records, they were allowed to leave without being arrested.

READ MORE

Wounded Knee, South Dakota, was the site of a notorious massacre in 1890. For details, see page 53.

The next year, protesters took over the village of Wounded Knee, South Dakota, on the reservation where Russell had been born. Russell and the other demonstrators wanted to protest the way the president of the reservation ruled. They said he ignored poverty and other problems. They also claimed he used his power abusively. The protesters held Wounded Knee for 71 days. Outsiders sent in food and supplies. The Indians and the government discussed

Russell Means prepares for the Wounded Knee takeover, March 1973.

the situation, but talks broke down. The sides exchanged gunfire, and two protesters were killed. When the occupation ended, little changed on the reservation. However, the publicity made the nation aware of Indians' problems. Russell believed the protest helped his people regain their dignity.

Changing Directions

After Wounded Knee, Russell continued to get involved in protests. He served time in prison for taking part in a riot. His anger spilled over into his personal life. Often involved in fights, he was shot three times and stabbed once. His second marriage ended, and he married and divorced two more times. He had 10 children but admitted that he wasn't a good father. In 1999, when he was 60, Russell married his fifth wife, Pearl. She is half Navajo and half white.

Even while protesting, Russell wanted to do something to help preserve the culture of his people, the Lakota Sioux. In the 1990s, Russell found a new way to help white Americans understand Indian culture. He began to act in movies, including *Pocahontas*. One of his best-known roles was as the wise, calm father Chingachgook in *The Last of the Mohicans* (1992). He also acted in television shows. Some people criticized Russell for playing Hollywood Indians, but he believed that the roles helped correct false images from the past.

One important way to preserve culture is to pass it along to young people. To do this, Russell and his wife plan to start a school, called the TREATY Total Immersion School. It will use traditional methods to teach Lakota children their language

READ MORE

The Last of the Mohicans, starring Russell Means and Daniel Day-Lewis, was a popular movie. For information about the book on which it was based, see page 54.

Russell Means announces the withdrawal of the "Lakotah Nation" from all treaties with the United States, December 19, 2007. Russell has remained uncompromising in his demands for Indian rights.

and culture. In an article in the magazine *The Santa Fean*, Russell used an African proverb to explain his goals: "There's a saying in West Africa, 'It takes a village to educate a child.' That's what we're going to do—nurture well-rounded human beings, teach them how to get along with everyone."

Russell has not lost his anger about the problems that Indians face. In late 2007, he sent a letter to the U.S. government and the states of Montana, Wyoming, North Dakota, South Dakota, and Nebraska. In it, he announced that a nation called Lakotah had reclaimed its traditional lands and set up its own government. Other Sioux leaders claimed that Russell had no right to take such an action. No tribal governments backed his plan. But the disapproval didn't stop Russell Means. He intends to do anything he can to win rights for American Indians.

CHAPTER SEVEN

DAVID SALMON: ATHABASCAN CHIEF AND CHRISTIAN PRIEST

On October 15, 2007, the day that Chief David Salmon's funeral was held, state flags across Alaska were lowered to half-mast in his honor. David was an elder of the Gwich'in people, an Athabascan group. He was also an ordained priest of the Episcopal Church. Alaska's governor, Sarah Palin, said in an official statement, "Alaska has lost a true treasure. Chief Salmon will be remembered as an inspiration to all Alaskans."

David's friends remembered him as a quiet, humble man who was quick to laugh. Why was this quiet man's life inspiring to so many people?

Raised the Traditional Way

In 1912, David was born to William and Alice Salmon, in Salmon Village in northern Alaska near the Canadian border. In 1923, when David was 10 or 11 years old, he killed his first moose and his first caribou. That same year, his mother died of tuberculosis. At that time, no cure existed for tuberculosis, which was widespread

READ MORE

For information about the history and teachings of the Episcopal Church, see page 55.

David Salmon, Gwich'in elder and First Traditional Chief of the Interior of Alaska, speaks at a conference in Anchorage, October 2006.

in the village. William Salmon wanted to save his son from the disease, so he sent him to a boarding school in Fort Yukon.

David stayed there for two years, finishing first and second grade. Then his father came to pick him up. William Salmon had bought enough supplies to last an entire year. Loading everything onto a motorboat, William took his son up the Black River far into the wilderness where no people lived.

For the next 18 years, the Salmons lived in what William called "No Man's Land." In winter, the temperatures could drop to 50 degrees below zero. William taught David traditional Athabascan skills, such as toolmaking and canoe building. He also passed on stories and legends that he had learned from his own father. The two hunted by running a trapline. They stayed in the backcountry for more than 10 months at a time, and then they would travel by boat to Fort Yukon. There they would sell the furs they took from the animals they trapped. They used the money to buy food and supplies for the next year.

On one of those trips to town, David married a woman named Sarah. The couple lived in the backcountry, where Sarah taught David how to read and write English. He already knew how to read and write his Athabascan language. David and Sarah would be married for 59 years. They had one son and adopted a daughter. They also had five grandchildren and 12 great-grandchildren.

Becoming Chief and Priest

In 1941, David and his wife moved to the village of Chalkyitsik on the Black River. They wanted to help build up the community, so David constructed a log school by hand. He became chief of the village, an elected position.

Even after many years in the wilderness, David still cared deeply about the Episcopal Church. In the mid-1950s, he began to talk to Walter Hannum, a minister in Fort Yukon, about becoming a minister himself. At the same time, David and several other villagers began to construct a large log church in Chalkyitsik.

The Episcopal Church sent David to Bible schools in Michigan and New York. When he returned to Alaska, he studied for another year with Hannum. In 1958, he was ordained as a deacon in the Episcopal Church. A deacon is a minister who may preach but may not bless the bread and wine at communion.

For four years after that, David flew to villages around Alaska helping other ministers to hold services. During that time, he continued to study. In 1962, he was ordained as a priest. About that time, he helped to found the Tanana Chiefs Conference, which serves the health and social service needs of Alaska Natives.

For five years, David worked as the priest of a church in Venetie, Alaska. He preached his sermons in his native language.

After that, he served in Fort Yukon for three years, went to college in Arizona for two years, and then returned to the church in Chalkyitsik. He served there nine years and then retired.

In addition to teaching about God, David Salmon also worked to preserve his native culture. He passed on the stories and music of his people to the next generation. He held classes in how to make and use Athabascan tools such as bows, arrows, and spears. He constructed many birchbark canoes, which are on display throughout Alaska. David also worked with a writer to record the oral history his father had passed on to him. As David explained, "The history of this country is not known. Young people do not know it. Old people die with it. Well, I don't want to die with it. I want the young people to have it."

In 2004, David was named Alaska's First Traditional Chief of the Interior. This non-elected office is a position of high honor. In 2007, he was diagnosed with cancer. According to his granddaughter, he died at home, sitting in his favorite chair.

Steve Ginnis, president of the Tanana Chiefs Conference—a group David Salmon helped found to promote the welfare of Native Alaskans—attends a hearing on land management issues.

CROSS-CURRENTS

Powwows

Indians who have attended the National Powwow view the event as a way to celebrate and display American Indian culture. The term *powwow* is believed to have come from the Narragansett Indians, who lived in Rhode Island. It probably referred to a healer or a healing ritual. Various Indian tribes had ceremonies that could be called powwows.

White traders who traveled the country selling medicine picked up the term and used it to describe their products. To attract customers, the traders put on "medicine shows" featuring hired Indian dancers. Soon the term *powwow* came to mean the act of dancing in front of an audience. That is how the name is used today. One way that modern powwows are different from Indian dances of the past is that people from many tribes take part. In past times, each tribe held its own private dances.

Two young Indians dance at the first National Powwow, Washington, D.C., August 2005.

Tribal Membership

Different tribes use different methods to determine who is allowed to be listed as a member. The most common method is to calculate how much Indian blood a person has. For many tribes, a person cannot be a member unless he or she is at least one-quarter Indian. This method can lead to problems. For example, if a man's parents come from different tribes, he might not have enough ancestry to be accepted by either tribe.

Some tribes believe culture is more important than ancestry. They look at factors such as whether the person has lived on the reservation or speaks the native language. As more Indians move off the reservation and marry people from other tribes, the definitions of tribal membership may have to change.

A Sioux family, circa 1899. Today, various methods are used to determine who is eligible to claim membership in a particular tribe.

CROSS-CURRENTS

Judo

The sport of judo has its origins in jujitsu, a method of unarmed combat that was used in Japan. In 1882, a Japanese teacher named Jigoro Kano developed judo—which means "gentle way"—as a safe form of jujitsu. He intended judo to be a method of physical education.

The goal of judo is to throw or pin an opponent cleanly. The moves are designed to use an opponent's force and turn it against him or her.

People who practice judo are expected to be courteous toward their opponents. When competing, they wear a white jacket and trousers and are barefoot. Belts of various colors indicate what level of skill a judo practitioner has reached.

The year 1964 was the first year that judo was an Olympic sport. That was also the year that Ben Nighthorse Campbell competed. Since then, judo has become increasingly popular and more competitive.

Judo moves are designed to take advantage of an opponent's momentum.

The Battle of the Little Bighorn

The Little Bighorn is a river in Montana. On June 25, 1876, a major battle was fought along its banks.

An 1868 treaty had given Indians ownership of the Dakota Territory. However, white miners looking for gold trespassed on the land. In response, Indians raided white settlements. The U.S. government viewed that as breaking the treaty. So in 1876, it sent troops against the Indians.

General Alfred Terry took a large force to the mouth of the Little Bighorn River. Lieutenant Colonel George A. Custer was supposed to lead a smaller force, the Seventh Cavalry, farther up the river. The plan was to trap the Indians between the two forces.

On his way, however, Custer came across a large camp of Plains Indians and decided to attack on his own. He divided his troops, planning to assault the camp from three directions. That decision proved to be a terrible mistake. The Indians repelled two of the Seventh Cavalry detachments. These men had to dig in to avoid being wiped out by the Indians. Several miles away, more than 200 troops led by Custer were surrounded. In about an hour's time, the Indians had killed Custer and all of his men.

Although the Battle of the Little Bighorn was a victory for the Plains Indians, it made white Americans furious. Many more U.S. Army troops were sent out to subdue the Indians. Within a year, they had succeeded.

Indians charge at the Little Bighorn.

Log Cabins

Log cabins are usually associated with the settlement of America's western frontier during the 1800s. However, log cabins were actually introduced into North America much earlier, and in the east. The first were built in the early 1700s (or perhaps the late 1600s) by Swedes who established a colony in what is now Delaware.

The log cabin became a favorite dwelling of frontier settlers for several reasons. First, settlers could construct log cabins using only materials they found on the land. They didn't even need nails, which were expensive. Second, building a log cabin could take as little as a few days, and it didn't require great skill. But these structures were snug and sturdy.

To build a log cabin, settlers would chop down trees with an ax and cut off the branches. Sometimes they would place the first logs on top of stones to prevent the logs from rotting. The logs were then stacked in a square or rectangular pattern. The ends of the logs were notched so the corners would fit together. After all the logs had been placed, the gaps between the logs were filled with homemade cement. A well-made log cabin could last for decades.

Swedish settlers introduced the log cabin to America in the late 1600s or early 1700s.

Eleanor Roosevelt (1884–1962)

Eleanor Roosevelt was a niece of President Theodore Roosevelt. Her family was wealthy, but they believed in helping others. As a young woman, Eleanor taught in a poor neighborhood.

When she was 21, she married her distant cousin, Franklin D. Roosevelt. He went into politics, serving as a state senator, secretary of the navy, and governor of New York. In 1921, he caught polio, which left him unable to walk. With Eleanor's help, he continued his political career. In 1932, in the midst of the nation's worst economic depression, Franklin Roosevelt was elected president. During her husband's 12 years in office, Eleanor worked tirelessly for many causes. She promoted equal rights for all, and she tried to help the poor. After Franklin's death in 1945, Eleanor became a delegate to the United Nations. When she died, she was one of the most admired women in the world.

Eleanor Roosevelt, circa 1933.

Ralph Nader

The son of Lebanese immigrants, Ralph Nader was born in 1934. He earned a law degree from Harvard University. In 1965, Nader gained national fame after his book *Unsafe at Any Speed* was published. In it, he criticized the automobile industry for producing cars with dangerous designs. The book helped bring about the passage of a car-safety law. After that, Nader became an advocate for consumers. He promoted the anti-nuclear movement, the environmental movement, and other issues.

In 1996 and 2000, Nader ran for president as the candidate of the Green Party. He knew he could not win, but his goal was to attract 5 percent of voters to the Green Party. Reaching that threshold would qualify the Green Party to receive government money in the next election. In both elections, however, Nader failed to get more than 3 percent of the vote. Nader also made unsuccessful runs for the presidency in 2004 and 2008, as an independent candidate.

Consumer advocate and activist Ralph Nader has run for U.S. president four times.

Rebuilding Postwar Europe

World War II was the deadliest conflict in history. Scholars estimate that 60 million people died in the war. Between 15 million and 20 million were killed in Europe alone. In addition, the war caused destruction on an almost unimaginable scale. Nearly every country in Europe was a battleground. Entire cities were turned into rubble by bombs dropped from airplanes. Buildings were flattened. Railroads, bridges, and roads were destroyed.

When the war ended in 1945, Europe was in a shambles. Millions of people were hungry and homeless. The continent's weak economies were unable to provide jobs or the goods people needed.

To help get Europe back on its feet, the United States created a massive rebuilding plan. It was called the Marshall Plan, after General George C. Marshall, the U.S. secretary of state who first proposed the plan. Between 1948 and 1951, the Marshall Plan provided more than $13 billion in aid to Western Europe. This included emergency food aid as well as money and technical assistance for rebuilding.

The program proved highly effective. Western Europe's economies were soon productive once again.

World War II left much of Europe in ruins. The Marshall Plan helped Western Europe recover and rebuild.

CROSS-CURRENTS

Jim Crow Laws

Beginning in the 1870s, many Southern states passed laws to keep the races separate. These were called Jim Crow laws after a character in a song-and-dance show that was a negative stereotype of African Americans. Jim Crow laws decreed that whites and blacks—and in some states, Indians—must have separate schools, parks, theaters, restaurants, and even cemeteries. They had to ride in separate sections of buses and trains. The laws did more than just segregate the races. They reserved the best facilities for whites. Throughout the South, the facilities set aside for African Americans and Indians were run-down and of poor quality. In the 1950s, civil rights activists began to attack Jim Crow laws by refusing to obey them. Today, Jim Crow restrictions are illegal in the United States.

Jim Crow was an offensive character representing black men in 19th-century song-and-dance shows. The name came to refer to the system of racial segregation in the South.

Wounded Knee

The South Dakota village that AIM protesters took over in 1973 was the site of one of the most notorious episodes in the history of the U.S. government's treatment of American Indians. During the late 1880s, a Paiute Indian named Wovoka experienced a vision in which he saw Indians being reunited with their dead ancestors and whites being swept away. To make this vision a reality, Wovoka said, Indians shouldn't fight with the whites. Rather, they should perform a ritual dance known as the Ghost Dance.

The Ghost Dance movement began to spread throughout the Sioux reservations of the Dakotas. Many whites became alarmed even though the Indians had not committed any violence against them. It was decided that Indian leaders should be arrested. On December 14, 1890, the famous Sioux chief Sitting Bull was killed when reservation police attempted to take him into custody. Afterward, a band of Sioux left their reservation and went to hide in the nearby Badlands, which was hilly country. The U.S. army went after them and surrounded their camp near Wounded Knee Creek. As the soldiers took the Indians' guns, a shot was fired accidentally. In response, the soldiers opened fire, even though most of the Indians were unarmed. It is estimated that at least 200 Indians were killed. Many of the dead were women and children.

Sitting Bull, whose killing in 1890 set in motion events that would end with the Wounded Knee massacre.

CROSS-CURRENTS

The Last of the Mohicans

The popular 1992 movie *The Last of the Mohicans* is based on a novel of the same name by American writer James Fenimore Cooper. Published in 1826, *The Last of the Mohicans* was the second in a series of five books called the Leatherstocking tales. The books follow the life and adventures of a fictional frontiersman and wilderness scout named Natty Bumppo.

The Last of the Mohicans is set during the French and Indian War. That war, fought in North America between 1754 and 1760, was part of a larger struggle between England and France. In North America, French soldiers, French colonists from Canada, and their Indian allies fought against British soldiers, British colonists, and other Indians. In *The Last of the Mohicans*, Natty and his fictional Indian friends Chingachgook and Uncas aid the British. The book also includes real characters, such as the French general Montcalm, as well as descriptions of actual events, such as the British surrender of Fort William Henry in 1757. However, historians agree that Cooper often exaggerated the facts.

While his Leatherstocking books were very popular during the 1800s, some critics fault Cooper for presenting an inaccurate and idealized picture of frontier life. Still, his sympathetic depiction of Indians was groundbreaking.

A page from an early printing of James Fenimore Cooper's *The Last of the Mohicans*.

The Episcopal Church

The Episcopal Church is part of the Anglican Communion, a family of churches associated with the Church of England. The Church of England, or Anglican church, was founded in the 1530s, after a dispute between King Henry VIII and the Roman Catholic pope. The pope refused to permit Henry to divorce his wife and marry another woman, so the British king had himself proclaimed the head of the Christian church in England.

Some, but not all, of the British colonists who settled in North America during the 1600s and 1700s were members of the Church of England. After the American Revolution, they formed the Episcopal Church in the United States. While it was separate from the Church of England, the Episcopal Church maintained core Anglican beliefs and traditions.

The Episcopal Church practices a blend of Catholic and Protestant traditions. Like the Catholic Church, it has a formal type of worship that includes communion every Sunday. Its ministers, like those of the Catholic Church, are called priests. However, unlike the Catholic Church but like other Protestant denominations, the Episcopal Church permits married clergy and allows women to be ordained into the ministry. The Episcopal Church's services are written out in the Book of Common Prayer.

King Henry VIII, whose dispute with the pope led to the founding of the Church of England.

Chronology

1890: The Wounded Knee massacre ends the Indian wars.

1924: American Indians are granted U.S. citizenship.

1934: The Indian Reorganization Act allows tribes to create their own governments.

1944: The National Congress of American Indians is formed.

1952: The U.S. government's relocation program begins to move Indians to cities.

1954: The termination policy begins.

1963: The terminated Menominee tribe is restored to official status.

1964: A group of Indians briefly occupies Alcatraz Island.

1968: The American Indian Movement (AIM) is founded.

1972: AIM leads a march on Washington and seizes the headquarters of the Bureau of Indian Affairs.

1973: AIM occupies Wounded Knee, South Dakota.

1978: A law is passed to protect Indian religious rights.

1988: A law is passed allowing tribes to run casinos on Indian land.

1990: A law is passed to protect Indian burial sites.

2004: The Smithsonian's National Museum of the American Indian opens.

2005: The Mississippi Choctaw reservation is damaged by Hurricane Katrina.

2006: The Navajo and the Hopi resolve a 40-year-old land dispute in Arizona.

2007: The U.S. government awards $1.5 million to 13 tribes to develop energy resources.

2008: The Department of the Interior signs an agreement with the Mashantucket and Seminole tribes to promote business development.

Further Reading

Books

Henry, Christopher E., and W. David Baird. *Ben Nighthorse Campbell: Cheyenne Chief and U.S. Senator.* New York: Chelsea House, 1995.

Lobb, Nancy. *16 Extraordinary Native Americans.* Portland, ME: Walch, 2007.

Silverstone, Michael. *Winona LaDuke.* New York: The Feminist Press at CUNY, 2001.

Sonneborn, Liz. *A to Z of American Indian Women.* New York: Facts on File, 2007.

Periodicals

Bordewich, Fergus. "How to Succeed in Business: Follow Choctaws' Lead." *Smithsonian* (March 1996), 32–41.

Ellis, David, and Vickie Bane. "Rites of Victory." *People* (November 30, 1992), 50–52.

Plummer, William. "Hearing His Own Drum." *People* (October 12, 1992), 63–70.

———. "Chief of Choctaw, Inc." *People* (October 4, 1999), 91–94.

Internet Resources

http://bioguide.congress.gov/scripts/biodisplay.pl?index=C000077

Ben Nighthorse Campbell's congressional biography contains a list of his accomplishments.

http://www.wisconsinhistory.org/topics/deer/

The Wisconsin Historical Society has a one-page biography of Ada Deer.

http://voices.cla.umn.edu/vg/Bios/entries/laduke_winona.html

This one-page biography of Winona LaDuke also lists her published works.

http://www.choctaw.org/economics/eco_history.htm

The Choctaw tribal government's Web site includes a history of the tribe's economic development.

http://www.imdb.com/name/nm0575184/

The Russell Means page at the Internet Movie Database lists his movies and gives a brief biography.

http://www.episcopalchurch.org/81831_91054_ENG_HTM.htm

The Episcopal Church published this obituary of David Salmon.

Glossary

activist—someone who takes action, such as a protest or strike, to try to bring about change.

annul—to declare invalid or not legal.

bankruptcy—the state of being legally declared unable to pay one's debts.

ecosystem—a community made up of the plants and animals that live in one environment.

GED—general equivalency diploma; a degree that is equal to a high school diploma.

G.I. Bill—a law that provided veterans of the U.S. armed forces with government help to pay for education and housing.

massacre—to kill a large number of people, particularly when they are incapable of defending themselves.

repeal—to revoke or abolish.

reservation—an area of land set aside for American Indians.

termination—the process of bringing something to an end.

trapline—a route on which a series of animal traps is set.

tuberculosis—a disease that causes damage to the tissue of the lungs.

Chapter Notes

Chapter 1 American Indians Today

p. 9: "Many Indians and Inuit . . ." Barry M. Pritzker, *Native America Today* (Santa Barbara, CA: ABC-CLIO, 1999), xi.

p. 10: "Never again will we attack . . ." Kevin Gover, "Let the Healing Begin," *Vital Speeches of the Day* (Mount Pleasant, SC: City News Publishing, 2000), 745.

p. 11: "We fought to instill pride . . ." Russell Means, *Where White Men Fear to Tread* (New York: St. Martin's Press, 1995), 541.

Chapter 2 Ben Nighthorse Campbell: A Warrior Senator

p. 12: "Every time I stopped . . ." Fred Morrow, "Campbell Fights Off Mugger," *Pueblo Chieftain* (March 22, 1991).

p. 12: "And I didn't want to . . ." Ibid.

p. 13: "I remember being . . ." David Ellis and Vickie Bane, "Rites of Victory," *People* (November 30, 1992): 50–52.

Chapter 3 Ada Deer: The Woman Who Took on Congress

p. 19: "Like my ancestors . . ." Ada Deer, "The Menominee Quest." In *After Columbus: The Smithsonian Chronicle of the North American Indians* by Herman J. Viola (New York: Orion Books, 1990), 236.

p. 22: "Like me, other Menominees . . ." Ibid.

Chapter 4 Winona LaDuke: Candidate for Vice President

p. 24: "America is the single . . ." Winona LaDuke, *The Winona LaDuke Reader* (Stillwater, MN: Voyageur Press, 2002), 258.

p. 26: "Who we are is . . ." Ibid., 62.

Chapter 5 Phillip Martin: Leading His People to Prosperity

p. 29: "I joined the Army Air . . ." Rudi Williams, "Former Sergeant Leads Destitute Tribe to Economic Prosperity, Self-Respect," *American Forces Press Service* (November 20, 2002). http://www.defenselink.mil/news/newsarticle.aspx?id=42477

p. 31: "You have a lot of . . ." Ibid.

p. 32: "I've been all over . . ." Fergus M. Bordewich, "How to Succeed in Business: Follow Choctaws' Lead," *Smithsonian* (March 1996).

Chapter 6 Russell Means: Protests and Controversy

p. 34: "Pocahontas is the finest movie . . ." Katie Arnold, "The Ways of Means," *The Santa Fean* (November 2005). http://www.santafean.com/features/the-ways-of-means

p. 36: "It was my first inkling . . ." Means, *Where White Men Fear to Tread*, 106.

p. 39: "There's a saying . . ." Arnold, "Ways of Means."

Chapter 7 David Salmon: Athabascan Chief and Christian Priest

p. 40: "Alaska has lost . . ." Office of the Governor, "Governor Palin Orders Flags Lowered for Native Leader," October 12, 2007. http://gov.state.ak.us/archive-53346.html

p. 43: "The history of this country . . ." Council of Athabascan Tribal Governments, "David Salmon," *Elders Gallery*. http://www.catg.org/gallery/elders/DavidSalmon.html

Index

Numbers in ***bold italics*** refer to captions.

Photo Credits

7: Tim Sloan/AFP/Getty Images
8: Peter Essick/Aurora/Getty Images (right); Robyn Beck/AFP/Getty Images (left)
13: Mario Tama/AFP/Getty Images
16: Acey Harper/Time Life Pictures/Getty Images
17: Mark Wilson/Getty Images
18: MPI/Getty Images
20: Bettmann/Corbis
21: Steven L. Raymer/National Geographic/Getty Images
23: AIS Associate Director Denise Wiyaka/University of Wisconsin
25: AP Photo/Chad Harder
28: AP Photo/Eric Miller
30: AP Photo/Rogelio Solis
33: AP Photo/Marcy Nighswander
35: AP Photo/The Daily Times/Benjamin Chrisman
36: Ralph Crane/Time Life Pictures/Getty Images
37: Dirck Halstead/Time & Life Pictures/Getty Images
39: AP Photo/Stephen J. Boitano
41: AP Photo/Anchorage Daily News, Bill Roth
43: AP Photo/Al Grillo
44: Paul J. Richards/AFP/Getty Images
45: Library of Congress
46: Used under license from Shutterstock, Inc.
47: Library of Congress
48: Used under license from Shutterstock, Inc.
49: Library of Congress
50: AP Photo/David Zalubowski
51: National Archives and Records Administration
52: Library of Congress
53: Library of Congress
54: Library of Congress
55: © 2008 Jupiterimages Corporation

Cover Images
Main Image: Mark Wilson/Getty Images
Top Inset: John M. Heller/Getty Images
Bottom Inset: MPI/Getty Images

About the Author

RUTH HULL CHATLIEN has worked as a writer and editor on literature and social studies textbooks for twenty years. U.S. history and world history are her two favorite subjects to write about. She has also published five short stories. This is her first book for young people. Ruth lives in Zion, Illinois, with her husband Michael and their dog Smokey.